BBC MUSIC GUIDE

BACH CANTATAS

J. A. WESTRUP

BRITISH BROADCASTING CORPORATION

00015087

Published by the British Broadcasting Corporation
35 Marylebone High Street, London W.1

ISBN: 0 563 06784 5

First published 1966
Reprinted 1968, 1972, 1975, 1978
© J. A. Westrup 1966

Printed in England by The Garden City Press Limited
Letchworth, Hertfordshire SG6 1JS

BACH CANTATAS

Bach was a practical composer. Most of his music was written because it was needed – to provide material for his pupils to practise, to add to the repertory of a students' orchestra, to celebrate a birthday, a wedding or a funeral, and to supply music for the principal Sunday service in the Lutheran church. He was very well aware of the occasions for which his music was required. Music for a nobleman or a royal person had to be pompous and ceremonial in character, but if it was too elaborate there was a danger of boredom. If we look at the cantatas written to celebrate the King of Poland and other members of the Saxon house we notice that all but one of the final choruses are extremely simple, straightforward music, with tunes which people could whistle afterwards; and even the exception includes very little that could be described as complicated. An additional reason for simplicity is that the performers were mainly students of Leipzig University and time for rehearsal was short. Each of these five cantatas is called by Bach a *dramma*, and in three of them the soloists represent mythological or symbolical characters. 'Lasst uns sorgen' (BWV 213)[1] shows us the youthful Hercules making the right choice between Pleasure and Virtue, with particular reference to the outstanding virtue of the young Crown Prince, whose birthday it was. In 'Tönet, ihr Pauken' (BWV 214), in honour of the Queen of Poland, the characters are Bellona, goddess of War, Pallas, Peace (a tenor) and Fame. In 'Schleicht, spielende Wellen' (BWV 206) all four soloists take the part of rivers – the Pleisse (one of the rivers on which Leipzig stands), the Danube, the Elbe and the Vistula. The title *dramma* should not mislead us into supposing that these works were acted: they were intended for concert performance. At the same time it is clear that Bach was thoroughly familiar with the operatic style of his time. His second son, Carl Philipp Emanuel, tells us that one of the composers whom he particularly admired was Johann Adolph Hasse, who was appointed director of the Dresden Opera in 1731; and Bach's biographer Forkel relates that he

[1] The letters BWV stand for *Bach-Werke-Verzeichnis*, a thematic catalogue compiled by Wolfgang Schmieder.

5

liked to take his eldest son, Wilhelm Friedemann, to Dresden to hear the opera there. His cantata 'Schweigt stille, plaudert nicht' (BWV 211), dealing with a father's objection to his daughter's passion for coffee, is in all essentials a miniature opera, though it employs a narrator. The same is true of 'Mer hahn en neue Oberkeet' (BWV 212), popularly known as the *Peasant Cantata*. Written partly in dialect, it represents the villagers' convivial welcome to the Saxon Court Chamberlain on his succession to his mother's estate. Here Bach wrote in a style which would not be out of place in a French *opéra-comique*, and he was not above introducing popular tunes, including a hunting song which he may have got from his friend Count Sporck, who was the first to introduce hunting-horns into Bohemia. (Needless to say the song includes an obbligato for the horn.) In works of this kind Bach made no attempt to be learned, though everything he wrote shows an infallible mastery of technique. And there are many other examples which only need to be known to be as popular as the air for Pales in the hunting cantata 'Was mir behagt' (BWV 208), which the mere accident of transcription has made familiar to music-lovers as 'Sheep may safely graze'.

Another link with opera was the use of recitative, which was employed also in church cantatas, mainly through the influence of Erdmann Neumeister (1671–1756), a Lutheran pastor and theologian, who began publishing texts to be set to music in 1700. The four cantatas which Bach wrote when he was a young organist at Mühlhausen (1707–8) belong to an older tradition and have no recitative. But from the time he resumed the composition of cantatas in Weimar in 1714 he used it constantly. Neumeister, some of whose texts were set by Bach, had made no bones about his view of the cantata: in his earliest collection he declared that it was in effect part of an opera, consisting of recitatives and arias. For this reason his earlier libretti were designed simply for soloists. But realizing, perhaps, that to exclude the chorus in works intended for the church was going too far, he subsequently widened the scope of his cantatas to include choral movements, hymns and texts taken from the Bible. In this way the church cantata became a mixture of the old traditions and the modern tendencies of the new century. Whether composers agreed with Neumeister or not that a cantata was an opera, the result was the same. There cannot be two ways of writing a recitative: the same formulas have to serve for joy in God and the praises of a prince, for a sinner's repentance and despair in love. People who have never heard an early eighteenth-century opera find this hard to believe, and in consequence the significance of the recitative in Bach's church cantatas (and the Passions too) is often over-estimated. This is not to deny that it covers quite a wide range of expression; but there is nothing specifically religious about it, and without the words no one would know whether it was intended for the theatre or the church. This can best be illustrated by two examples from Bach's own work. The first is from the secular cantata (or *dramma per musica*) 'Zerreisset, zersprenget, zertrümmert die Gruft' (BWV 205), performed at Leipzig in 1725 to celebrate the birthday of Professor August Friedrich Müller:

EX. I

(Dear Aeolus, pray do not upset our merry-making, since Helicon, home of my Muses, has organized a festival, a pleasant celebration, on its summit)

The second excerpt is from the *St Matthew Passion* (BWV 244):

EX. 2

(At that moment one of those with Jesus reached for his sword and drew it and struck at the High Priest's servant and cut off his ear)

As we have seen, Bach's earliest church cantatas were written at Mühlhausen (a town in Thuringia thirty miles north-west of Erfurt), where he was organist at the church of St Blasius from 1707 to 1708. His time there was too short for him to do much more than collect a repertory of church music by other composers. It is significant that all the four cantatas which he wrote during this year seem to have been intended for particular occasions, not for the regular services of the church. 'Aus der Tiefe' (BWV 131) is a penitential work which may, as Terry suggests, have been written to commemorate a disastrous fire which occurred in Mühlhausen in the summer of 1707. 'Gott ist mein König' (BWV 71) was performed, not in St Blasius's Church but in St Mary's, on the occasion of the election of a new town council on 4 February 1708. The vocal and instrumental parts of this work were printed – a unique experience in Bach's career, apart from a similar work (now lost) which is said to have been published in the following year. 'Der Herr denket an uns' (BWV 196) appears to have been written for a wedding, and 'Gottes Zeit ist die allerbeste Zeit' (BWV 106), described in the only surviving copy of the score as *actus tragicus*, is obviously intended for a funeral. The special occasion for which 'Gott ist mein König' was written made it possible for Bach to use unusually elaborate instrumental resources: two recorders, two oboes, bassoon, three trumpets, timpani and strings. The other three are much more modest in their requirements: 'Gottes Zeit' is written for a chamber ensemble consisting of two recorders, two bass viols and continuo (organ and cello). (Though Bach occasionally used the bass viol as a solo instrument, he used a pair of these instru-

8

ments in only two other works – the sixth Brandenburg concerto and a funeral ode for the Queen of Poland.) All four of the Mühlhausen cantatas use texts from the Bible, though not, with one exception, exclusively. 'Aus der Tiefe' is a setting of Psalm 130, 'Out of the deep have I called unto thee, O Lord'; 'Der Herr denket an uns' of Psalm 115, verses 12–15, beginning 'The Lord hath been mindful of us'. The other two draw on various Biblical sources, to which, in 'Gott ist mein König', are added two original sections in verse celebrating the new town council. There are no additions of any kind in 'Der Herr denket an uns', but in the other three Lutheran chorales (or hymns) are introduced. This is natural enough, since the chorale was an important element in the Lutheran service; and quite a number of Bach's later cantatas end with a reasonably simple setting of the tune, supported by all the instruments, in which the congregation could join. But even if the music was too elaborate for this, there was a good deal to be said for including one or more chorales which everyone would know, so that the congregation could feel themselves to be not merely listeners but also silent participants. For this reason a number of seventeenth-century composers used the chorale as the sole basis for a composition, setting the successive verses to varied treatment of the melody (a similar method was used in organ compositions). Bach himself did this in 'Christ lag in Todesbanden' (BWV 4), which probably dates from his years at Weimar. In 'Gottes Zeit', the third of the three Mühlhausen cantatas which we are considering, the work ends with an elaborate version of a chorale melody: there are instrumental interludes between the entries of the voices, the soprano sings an ornamented variant of the tune, and the last line is developed as a fugue. Elsewhere in these three cantatas a chorale melody is introduced as counterpoint to an aria; there are two examples in 'Aus der Tiefe' (both with words), one, ornamented, in 'Gott ist mein König', and two (one played by the recorders, the other with words) in 'Gottes Zeit'. The reason why there is no chorale in 'Der Herr denket an uns' may very well be that it was sung at a purely private ceremony.

After a year in Mühlhausen Bach decided that he needed more scope and also more money. In his letter of resignation he explained that an invitation to Weimar (which lies between Erfurt and Jena) offered him 'the possibility of a more adequate living and the achievement of my goal of a well-regulated church music without further vexation'.[1] It is understandable that he should have wanted to leave Mühlhausen, where both the opportunities and encouragement seem to have been limited. But his appointment to the Duke of Sachsen-Weimar in 1708 can hardly be said to have offered him immediately the opportunities he was looking for. His position was that of a *Cammermusicus*, i.e. an instrumentalist required to take part, either as a harpsichord player or as a violinist, in the small ensemble which the Duke maintained. Two years later he became court organist but still had no opportunity of exercising the profession which he said had drawn him to Weimar. He did, however, have plenty of time to perfect his organ-playing and to write a large number of works for the instrument. In view of his frustration it is hardly surprising that he was strongly tempted by the offer of a post at the Liebfrauenkirche in Halle, Handel's birthplace. But a change in his position at Weimar persuaded him to decline it: in March 1714 the Duke promoted him to be *Concertmeister*, with the specific duty of composing and performing a new work every month. A new series of cantatas began, but came to an abrupt end in 1716. In December of that year the Duke's *Capellmeister* (director of music), Johann Samuel Drese, died. Bach may reasonably have expected to succeed him, but instead the Duke appointed Drese's son. Once again Bach found his employment uncongenial. In August of the following year he accepted the post of *Capellmeister* to Prince Leopold of Anhalt-Cöthen. This move was not popular with the Duke, particularly as the Prince was the brother-in-law of his own nephew, whom he cordially detested. Bach was ordered to stay in Weimar. He refused and was kept in prison for a month, being finally released on 2 December 1717.

Assuming that Bach wrote one cantata a month he would have produced just over thirty between 1 March 1714 and 1 December 1716. This is quite a substantial figure. It would be too much to expect that they should all have survived; but there are twenty-three in existence today which were either certainly or very probably written during these two and a half years. The conditions

[1] Translation from *The Bach Reader*, ed. Hans T. David and Arthur Mendel (New York, 1945), p. 60. The original is in *Bach-Dokumente*, I, ed. Werner Neumann and Hans-Joachim Schulze (Kassel, 1963), p. 19.

under which they were performed are worth investigating. The Duke's musical establishment was very small by any standards. Lists for the years 1714 and 1716 show that there were six boys, not more than six adult singers, one or two bassoon players, three violinists, a double bass, and in addition six trumpeters and a timpanist. The trumpeters and timpanist were employed for ceremonial duties, but their presence enabled Bach to introduce them into cantatas for festal occasions, such as 'Christen, ätzet diesen Tag' (BWV 63), for Christmas Day, which has parts for four trumpets. One at least of his players must have been a virtuoso to have dealt with the appallingly difficult first trumpet part in the bass aria in 'Erschallet, ihr Lieder' (BWV 172), written for Whit Sunday. No oboes are mentioned in the official records; these were probably supplied from the ranks of the town musicians. Here again Bach must have had the services of an uncommonly good player for the wonderful obbligato to the aria 'Seufzer, Tränen, Kummer, Not' in 'Ich hatte viel Bekümmernis' (BWV 21). The string players were probably supplemented by Bach himself, and no doubt one of them played viola. 'Gleich wie der Regen und Schnee vom Himmel fällt' (BWV 18) requires four violas, but there are no violin parts, so one may assume that all the violinists were capable of doubling on the viola. The absence of any mention of a cellist in the official lists is curious. There is no doubt that one was needed regularly, quite apart from the places where the cello has an independent part or a solo; two of the cantatas actually have parts for two cellos. It is possible that one of the bassoon players in the 1714 list also played the cello: what is certain is that Bach never wrote for an instrument that was not there.

Bach's small choir at Weimar must have been quite a competent body, but as a rule he makes only modest demands on it: it is perhaps significant that in the more elaborate choruses there is a certain amount of doubling of the voices by instruments. Six out of the twenty-one cantatas call for nothing more from the chorus than the straightforward singing of a chorale, and in three of them there is no chorus at all. No doubt there were times when the boys were ill or on holiday, or time for rehearsal was limited, when Bach found it simpler to rely on his soloists. The abilities of his solo tenor may be guessed from the accompanied recitative in 'Gleich wie der Regen' and the aria

'Bäche von gesalznen Zähren' in 'Ich hatte viel Bekümmernis' –
both very demanding. The cantata 'Bereitet die Wege' (BWV 132)
for the fourth Sunday in Advent makes almost equal demands on
the soprano, not to mention the virtuosity required of the solo
violin in the concluding aria.

If Bach's decision to leave Mühlhausen is surprising, his
migration to Cöthen is even more curious. Cöthen (now spelt
Köthen), eighteen miles due north of Halle and sixty miles as the
crow flies from Weimar, was the seat of a prince who was a
Calvinist, though his mother was a Lutheran. This meant that Bach
would have no opportunity of writing or performing church
music. On the other hand, Prince Leopold was keenly interested
in music and a year or two before Bach's appointment had
organized a small orchestra of professional players, to whom
were added visiting musicians from time to time. Two of these
visitors during Bach's period of office were horn-players, whose
skill is perpetuated in the first Brandenburg concerto. So far
as we know Bach had only once before had the opportunity of
writing for a pair of horns – in the hunting cantata already
mentioned, 'Was mir behagt', which was written in honour of
the birthday of Duke Christian of Sachsen-Weissenfels and
performed at Weissenfels (eighteen miles south of Halle) either
in 1713 or in 1716.[1] He was to use horns again frequently in the
cantatas, both sacred and secular, written at Leipzig, and he did
not forget the characteristic hunting calls which he had introduced both in 'Was mir behagt' and in the concerto.

Deprived of the opportunity of writing church music at Cöthen
Bach turned his attention to instrumental music. To this period
belong many of his best-known works for the harpsichord or
clavichord, the violin, the flute, the bass viol, the cello and the
orchestra. He was also able to pay tribute to his employer by
celebrating his birthday and the New Year with at least four, and
probably several more, cantatas. Only two of these survive: 'Die
Zeit, die Tag und Jahre macht' (BWV 134a) for New Year's Day,
1719, and 'Durchlauchtster Leopold' (BWV 173a), a birthday
cantata of uncertain date. (The former is referred to by older
writers as 'Mit Gnaden bekröne', which is the third line of the
aria which follows the opening recitative, 'Die Zeit, die Tag'.

[1] The date is discussed by Alfred Dürr in the *Kritischer Bericht* to Ser I,
vol. 35 of the new edition of Bach's works (Kassel, 1964), pp. 39–43.

The reason for this is that the opening pages are missing from the original score: the text, however, exists in a printed form, and the music can be reconstructed from other sources.) The first is a dialogue for Divine Providence (alto) and Time (tenor), with a chorus of congratulation at the end. The second includes a curious duet which begins in G major, continues in D major and ends in A major. It is marked 'Al tempo di minuetto', and the extended instrumental ritornellos suggest that some kind of ballet took place during the performance: one gets the same impression from the final movement, which is marked 'Chorus' but is in fact a duet for soprano and bass. Both these cantatas were to prove very useful to Bach when he was writing church cantatas at Leipzig.

After the death of his first wife on 4 July 1720 Bach may have felt that he needed a change of occupation; or perhaps the restlessness which he had felt at Mühlhausen and Weimar, and which he was to feel again at Leipzig, prompted him to consider leaving Cöthen. In the autumn he applied for the post of organist of St James's Church, Hamburg, where Erdmann Neumeister was the pastor; but the auditions were fixed so late in November that he was unable to attend on account of the Prince's birthday celebrations less than a fortnight later. In spite of this the committee, dissatisfied with the candidates, offered the post to Bach, but by this time he had decided not to accept. One of the reasons may well have been, as Mattheson suggested, that the successful applicant was expected to make a substantial contribution to church funds on his appointment. A year later Bach married his second wife, Anna Magdalena. The following week the Prince also married, but this was a less fortunate circumstance for the composer. The new princess was completely unmusical, and her lack of interest seems to have damped her husband's enthusiasm. Bach's thoughts began to turn towards other possibilities of employment, encouraged no doubt by the realization that he would soon be having a second batch of children to bring up.

Six months after Bach's marriage the death was announced of Johann Kuhnau, Cantor of the Thomasschule in Leipzig, and director of music in the two principal churches and the University church. One of the candidates for the post was Georg Philipp Telemann, but he withdrew in the autumn of 1722. It was only after this that Bach entered the field. One of the conditions imposed on the applicants was that they should compose substantial works and direct their performance in St Thomas's Church. Bach was asked to write a setting of the Passion for Good Friday, 1723. This was the origin of the *St John Passion*, a far more ambitious work than he had ever undertaken before but not materially different in style from his cantatas. The council had decided to elect Christoph Graupner, *Capellmeister* at Darmstadt, but his employer would not release him. They then proceeded unanimously to elect Bach, one member expressing the hope that he would not write theatrical music. Bach's official appointment dated from 5 May 1723. He must have received it with mixed feelings. He was well aware that he was the third choice, and he was under no illusion that his new post meant promotion. In eighteenth-century eyes a court *Capellmeister* was much more important than a music master in a school, even though he was also director of music to the University. But there were other considerations, among them the education of his sons, the eldest of whom, Wilhelm Friedemann, was nearly thirteen. Whatever the pros and cons, the decision was made. For the next twenty-seven years Leipzig was Bach's home.

The Thomasschule included day-boys, who followed a normal school curriculum, and a limited number of boarders who provided the choirs for three churches – St Thomas, St Nicholas and the New Church – and enough voices to sing the chorales at St Peter's. When Bach was appointed there were sixty-one of these singing boys, whose ages ranged from eleven to seventeen. Under his cantorship the upper age-limit rose as high as twenty-one. The boys, in fact, were not only trebles: they also included altos, tenors and basses. Among those whom Bach admitted in 1729 was one aged nineteen, described by him as a good sight-reader with a fine tenor voice. As time went on he became increasingly dissatisfied with the standard of singing. In a memorandum dated 23 August 1730 he described seventeen of them as fit for use, twenty as needing further training, and seventeen as quite incompetent. There was also the problem of instrumental players. The *Stadtpfeifer* (town wind-players) supplied two trumpeters and two oboists, there were three professional violinists, and there was an apprentice who played the bassoon. The other parts (including viola, cello and double bass) had to be supplied by a few students from the University or by members of the choir, who were naturally unable to sing when they were playing. It is difficult to know how this situation had arisen. Bach blamed the authorities, but it is not impossible that his own temperament was one of the reasons: he was certainly not an easy man to get on with. The depression which he felt at this time at the inadequacy of his resources is reflected in the letter which he wrote in October of the same year to his old friend Georg Erdmann, asking if there was any possibility of a post of some kind in Danzig. In addition to his difficulties at the Thomasschule he complains of the cost of living, which apparently was much higher in Leipzig than in his native Thuringia. Funerals, he remarks grimly, bring in an additional income, but unfortunately when there is a healthy breeze the number drops. It is worth noting that only a relatively small proportion of his church cantatas were written after the summer of 1727. Perhaps he had lost heart, or else had decided that he had enough in hand to see him through the rest of his time.

Cantatas were sung either at St Thomas's or at St Nicholas's by what was known as the first choir (*primus chorus*) of the Thomasschule: at the great festivals they were sung at both, which meant two separate performances. The normal place for the cantata was at the *Hauptgottesdienst*, the principal service of the day: when a second performance was required it was given at Vespers. The *Hauptgottesdienst* began at seven o'clock in the morning and lasted for several hours (the sermon alone was expected to last from eight to nine). It was a Communion service and hence included the two items of the Ordinary of the Mass which Luther had retained from the Roman Church – the *Kyrie* and the *Gloria*. They were known as the *Missa* (Mass) – the title given by Bach to the first two movements of what is known as the B minor Mass. The order of service varied in details according to the season, but the general plan was as follows:

1. Organ voluntary or hymn
2. Latin motet or organ voluntary
3. *Missa* (*Kyrie* and *Gloria*)
4. 'The Lord be with you', etc.
5. Latin collect
6. Epistle (intoned), followed by an organ interlude
7. Litany (omitted at certain festivals)
8. Hymn (appropriate to the season)
9. Gospel (intoned)

10. *Credo* (intoned in Latin; omitted when there was a cantata)
11. Cantata (described as *Stück* or *Concerto*; omitted in most of Advent and Lent)
12. The hymn 'Wir glauben all" (Luther's metrical version of the Creed)
13. Hymn before the sermon (followed by the gospel read in German)
14. Sermon
15. Banns of marriage
16. Prayers
17. Intercessions and notices
18. Hymn (related to the gospel)
19. The Lord's Prayer (intoned)
20. Prayer of consecration and Communion (during which hymns or a Latin motet might be sung)
21. Collects (intoned)
22. Blessing (intoned)

Sometimes the cantata was in two parts, in which case the second part was sung after the intercessions and notices instead of the hymn (No. 18). There are examples of this in Bach's works, for instance 'Herz und Mund und Tat und Leben' (BWV 147), which was originally composed at Weimar and revised later for use at Leipzig. Here each part ends with a verse of the same chorale, set to the same music and familiar to English music-lovers as 'Jesu, joy of man's desiring'. The text of the cantata, like the hymn after the intercessions, was always related to the gospel or the epistle for the day. Thus the Epiphany cantata 'Sie werden aus Saba alle kommen' (BWV 65) alludes to the story of the Wise Men as told in Matthew ii. 1-12. It begins with a quotation from Isaiah lx. 6: 'All they from Sheba shall come: they shall bring gold and incense; and they shall show forth the praises of the Lord', and follows this with the second verse ('Die Kön'ge aus Saba kamen dar') of the Christmas hymn 'Ein Kind geborn zu Bethlehem' (a translation of the old Latin hymn 'Puer natus in Bethlehem'). After this the emphasis is on the Christian's own offering. Material gifts are nothing: Jesus asks for the soul's surrender. 'Nimm mich dir zu eigen hin' (Take me for thine own) sings the tenor soloist; and the final chorale (a verse of Paul Gerhardt's 'Ich hab' in Gottes Herz und Sinn') echoes his words

> Ei nun, mein Gott, so fall' ich dir
> Getrost in deine Hände.
> Nimm mich, und mach' es so mit mir
> Bis an mein letztes Ende . . .

> (So now, Lord, with cheerful heart I fall into thy hands.
> Take me and stand beside me till my life ends.)

16

According to the official obituary of Bach, written by his son Carl Philipp Emanuel in collaboration with Johann Friedrich Agricola (a former pupil), he wrote five complete sets of cantatas for all the Sundays and holy days of the year. Since at Leipzig cantatas were not sung on the last three Sundays in Advent nor in Lent (except when the Feast of the Annunciation was transferred to Palm Sunday), this reduces the total number of Sunday cantatas in a year to forty-three. There were sixteen holy days on which cantatas were sung, so that the complete total for the year would be fifty-nine: in other words Bach wrote two hundred and ninety-five church cantatas. It is not clear whether C. P. E. Bach is referring only to cantatas written at Leipzig; but even if he is including those dating from Mühlhausen and Weimar, it is obvious that a good many must have been lost through the carelessness of those to whom they were entrusted, since we now possess less than two hundred. Even so, this is a substantial total; and since Bach was expected to produce a cantata for practically every Sunday, the burden of his early years in Leipzig must have been very heavy, especially as he not only wrote the scores but also copied a good many of the parts himself. There were two ways of lightening this burden. One was to use, with or without revisions, the cantatas which he had written at Weimar. Twenty of them, in fact, were revived at Leipzig – nineteen of them probably in his first year at the Thomasschule. The other solution was to make adaptations of his secular cantatas, either in whole or in part, and to use material from his instrumental works.

The idea of adapting secular material to make a church cantata is liable to shock people who believe that music for Divine Service should be 'devotional'. In practice it is quite impossible to make any distinction between the idioms of secular and sacred music: secular music in church sounds inappropriate only when it has purely secular associations. We have noticed already that there is no material difference between the recitatives in Bach's secular works and those in his church cantatas, oratorios and Passions. The same is true of his arias and choruses. Hence it was perfectly easy for him to adapt new words to music which originally had served quite a different purpose. It is obvious that this practice makes nonsense of the theory propounded by Schweitzer and other writers that Bach's music is infused with

17

symbolism and that all his settings are intimately related to the words (see p. 56). A simple example will illustrate this. The duet 'al tempo di minuetto' in the secular cantata 'Durchlauchtster Leopold' (BWV 173a), written at Cöthen, has already been mentioned. After a twelve-bar instrumental introduction the bass soloists sings the tune to the words (*a*):

EX. 3

(Under his purple robe joy follows sorrow: to one and all he gives ample scope.)

It was probably in 1724, at the end of his first year in Leipzig, that Bach turned most of this cantata into a church cantata for Whit Monday – 'Erhöhtes Fleisch und Blut' (BWV 173). The gospel for the day is John iii. 16 – 21, beginning: 'For God so loved the world, that he gave his only begotten son, that whosoever believeth in him should not perish, but have everlasting life.' Our duet now refers directly to this text (Ex.3 *b*): 'God so loved the world – his pity helps us in our need – that he gives us his son.' Whether or not we feel that the minuet rhythm is appropriate to these new words, it is impossible to argue that the music is inspired by them or in any way intimately related to them. This does not necessarily mean that Bach has committed an error of taste: on the contrary it is evidence of his skill and acumen in making these adaptations that most people, not knowing the original, would not feel any discomfort when listening to this cantata. Indeed, it is not unknown for innocent people to believe that 'Sheep may safely graze' comes from a cantata dealing with the Good Shepherd.

It was natural for Bach to use his secular cantatas as a source, since once they had been performed they were unlikely to be heard again with the same words. In some cases he did not hesitate to repeat a secular cantata with new words to suit a different occasion. When in 1734 he had to write a cantata to celebrate the coronation of the King of Poland, 'Blast Lärmen, ihr Feinde' (BWV 205a), he called to mind the *dramma per musica* which he had written for Professor Müller's birthday in 1725, 'Zerreisset, zersprenget' (BWV 205), perhaps because both the professor and the king were called August. It was a simple matter to adapt the recitatives, where necessary, to the new text: everything else was plain sailing, so that the chorus which had previously sung:

> Vivat August, August vivat!
> Sei beglückt, geehrter Mann

(Long live Augustus! Greetings to you, honoured sir)

could now exclaim with equal fervour and to the same music:

> Vivat August, August vivat!
> Bis der Bau der Erden fällt.

(Long live Augustus till the whole structure of the earth subsides!)

But adroit as he was at adaptation, Bach never (so far as we know) used the music of a church cantata for a secular one. (The funeral music for Prince Leopold (BWV 244a), 1728, which uses nine movements from the *St Matthew Passion*, can hardly be described as a secular cantata.)

Here are some examples of adaptations from secular sources, divided into those which derive from cantatas and those which use instrumental movements. The dates on the left (not always certain) are those of the church cantatas, on the right of the works from which music has been taken:

CHURCH CANTATAS	SECULAR CANTATAS
1724? 'Erfreut euch, ihr Herzen (BWV 66)	'Der Himmel dacht auf 1718 Anhalts Ruhm' (BWV 66a; music lost) [1]
1724 'Ein Herz, das seinen Jesum lebend weiss' (BWV 134)	'Die Zeit, die Tag und Jahre 1719 macht' (BWV 134a)
1724 'Erhöhtes Fleisch und Blut' (BWV 173)	'Durchlauchtster Leopold' 1722? (BWV 173a)

[1] The difference in metre is explained by the fact that Bach appears to have used the final chorus of BWV 66a ('Es strahle die Sonne') as the opening chorus of BWV 66.

1725	'Kommt, eilet und laufet' (BWV 249, *Easter Oratorio*)	'Entfliehet, verschwindet' 1725 (BWV 249a)
1731	'Schwingt freudig euch empor' (BWV 36)	'Scnwingt freudig euch 1725 empor' (BWV 36c)[1]
1738?	'Freue dich, erlöste Schar' (BWV 30)	'Angenehmes Wiederau' 1737 (BWV 30a)

CHURCH CANTATAS	INSTRUMENTAL WORKS
1725 'Unser Mund sei voll Lachens (BWV 110), opening chorus	Suite No. 4 in D major for 1721? orchestra (BWV 1069), overture
1726 'Geist und Seele wird verwirret' (BWV 35), opening *sinfonia*	Lost violin concerto in D 1721? minor, presumed original of a fragmentary harpsichord concerto in the same key (BWV 1059)[2]
1726 'Gott soll allein mein Herze haben' (BWV 169), opening *sinfonia* and alto aria (No. 5)	Lost violin concerto in E 1721? major (?), presumed original of harpsichord concerto in E major (BWV 1053), first and second movements[3]
1726 'Ich geh' und suche mit Verlangen' (BWV 49), opening *sinfonia*	E major concerto (see previous entry), third movement
1726 'Falsche Welt, dir trau' ich nicht' (BWV 52), opening *sinfonia*	Brandenburg concerto No. 1 in F major (BWV 1046), first 1721 movement
1727? 'Wir müssen durch viel Trübsal in das Reich Gottes eingehen' (BWV 146), opening *sinfonia* and chorus (No. 2)	Lost violin concerto in D 1721? minor, presumed original of harpsichord concerto in the same key (BWV 1052a), first and second movements
1728 'Ich steh' mit einem Fuss im Grabe' (BWV 156), opening *sinfonia*	Lost violin concerto in 1721? G minor (?), presumed original of the harpsichord concerto in F minor (BWV 1056), second movement

[1] This work was also used for two other secular cantatas: 'Steigt freudig in die Luft' (BWV 36a), for the birthday of the second wife of Prince Leopold of Anhalt-Cöthen, 1726, and 'Die Freude reget sich' (BWV 36b), for the birthday of a Leipzig citizen named Rivinus, 1735?

[2] It seems very likely that the opening *sinfonia* of Part II of the cantata comes from the finale of this concerto.

[3] Some modern writers maintain that this concerto was originally written for the harpsichord.

| 1729 | 'Ich liebe den Höchsten von ganzem Gemüte' (BWV 174), opening *sinfonia* | Brandenburg concerto No.172 3 in G major (BWV 1048), first movement |
| 1731 | 'Wir danken dir Gott' (BWV 29), opening *sinfonia*[1] | Partita in E major for violin1720 solo (BWV 1006), prelude |

It will be noticed that these adaptations, of which this not a complete list, are spread over a fairly wide period, suggesting that Bach made them only when he was pressed for time. On the other hand it should be remembered that a good many of his earlier works are lost. It is very possible that there are far more adaptations in the Leipzig cantatas than can be proved from circumstantial evidence. In particular many of the solos for which there is no pre-existing text sound as if they had originally been instrumental compositions or composed to other words. Though many of the borrowings from instrumental works are for the purpose of providing orchestral introductions to the cantatas, this is not invariably the case: see, for example, 'Unser Mund sei voll Lachens', 'Gott soll allein mein Herze haben' and 'Wir müssen durch viel Trübsal' in the above list. There are no good reasons for doubting the authenticity of this last cantata or the concerto from which it borrows.

Particularly interesting are the adaptations which Bach made in the *Christmas Oratorio* (BWV 248)[2]. This work consists of six cantatas, designed for Christmas Day, St Stephen's Day (Boxing Day), St John the Evangelist's Day, Feast of the Circumcision (New Year's Day), Sunday after New Year's Day, and Epiphany. It was performed during the Christmas season December 1734–January 1735. Though it was normal to perform cantatas on these days the production of such an elaborate series of related works must have presented a laborious task, particularly as by this time Bach had got out of the habit of working under the heavy pressure which had driven him on during his first three or four years in Leipzig. Fortunately there were two festal works immediately available – 'Lasst uns sorgen'

[1] Used again as the opening *sinfonia* of Part II of the wedding cantata 'Herr Gott, Beherrscher alle Dinge' (BWV 120a), 1732?

[2] Terry, in *Bach: a Biography* (London, 1928; 2nd ed. 1933), argued that the secular cantatas borrowed from the oratorio, not the other way about. These arguments were accepted by Whittaker in his posthumous work *The Cantatas of Johann Sebastian Bach, Sacred and Secular*, 2 vols. (London, 1959), but they fly in the face of all the evidence. See further, pp. 43-4.

(BWV 213), written to celebrate the birthday of the Crown Prince of Saxony on 5 September 1733, and 'Tönet, ihr Pauken' (BWV 214) for the birthday of the Queen of Poland on 8 December 1733. Both of these supplied a good deal of material for Parts I–IV of the oratorio. In Part V Bach borrowed a solo from a more recent work – the *dramma per musica* 'Preise dein Glücke' (BWV 215) for the anniversary of the king's accession (5 October 1734). By the time he came to Part VI he had no hesitation in incorporating a previous church cantata, now lost (BWV 248a), the opening chorus of which had already been used in a lost birthday cantata of 1731 (BWV Anh. 10). (The evidence for this is to be found in four of the original orchestral parts, which were obviously copied in the first place for a shorter, earlier work.) Here, in outline, are the details (without reference to any transpositions of the music):

CHRISTMAS ORATORIO	SECULAR CANTATAS
Part I	
1. Chorus: 'Jauchzet, frohlocket'	BWV 214, 1: 'Tönet, ihr Pauken'
4. Alto solo: 'Bereite dich Zion'	BWV 213, 9: 'Ich will dich nicht hören' (Hercules)
8. Bass solo: 'Grosser Herr'	BWV 214,7: 'Kron' und Preis'(Fame)
Part II	
15. Tenor solo: 'Frohe Hirten, eilt, ach eilet'	BWV 214, 5; 'Frommer Musen! Meine Glieder!' (Pallas, alto)
19. Alto solo: 'Schlafe, mein Liebster'	BWV 213: 3: 'Schlafe, mein Liebster' (Pleasure, soprano)
Part III	
24. Chorus: 'Herrscher des Himmels'	BWV 214, 9: 'Blühet, ihr Linden'
29. Duet (soprano and bass): 'Herr, dein Mitleid'	BWV 213, 11: 'Ich bin deine' (Hercules, alto; Virtue, tenor)
Part IV	
36. Chorus: 'Fallt mit Danken'	BWV 213, 1: 'Lasst uns sorgen'
39. Soprano solo (with echo): 'Flösst, mein Heiland'	BWV 213, 5: 'Treues Echo' (Hercules alto, with echo)
41. Tenor solo: 'Ich will nur dir zu Ehren leben'	BWV 213, 'Auf meinen Flügeln sollst du schweben' (Virtue)
Part V	
47. Bass solo: 'Erleucht' auch meine finstre Sinnen'	BWV 215, 7: 'Durch die von Eifer entflammeten Waffen' (soprano)

Part VI

54. Chorus: 'Herr, wenn die stolzen Feinde schnauben'

BWV Anh. 10, 1: 'So kämpfet nun, ihr muntern Töne' (*via* the opening chorus of BWV 248a.)

The opening chorus of the *Christmas Oratorio* is a good example of Bach's habit of borrowing material without worrying overmuch about its original associations. Everyone who has heard the oratorio will remember that it begins with a solo for the timpani – a unique occurrence in Bach's work. The reason for this is simple when we look at the chorus from which it is taken:

> Tönet, ihr Pauken! Erschallet, Trompeten!
> Klingende Saiten, erfüllet die Luft!
> Singet itzt Lieder, ihr muntren Poeten,
> Königin lebe! wird fröhlich geruft.
>
> (Beat, kettle-drums! Blow, trumpets!
> Sounding strings, fill the air!
> You cheerful poets, sing now your songs.
> 'Long live the Queen!' is the joyful cry.)

The ceremonial drums and trumpets have the first say, since this is a ceremonial celebration. It would be untrue to say that they are entirely out of place in a chorus celebrating the birth of Christ, but the manner in which they are introduced is certainly unusual.

Bach began his duties in Leipzig on the first Sunday after Trinity, 30 May 1723, when, we are told, he produced his first cantata 'with great success'. In his first year, as we have seen, he probably revived nineteen cantatas which he had written at Weimar and adapted three of the secular cantatas composed at Cöthen. One of his cantatas – 'Jesu nahm zu sich die Zwölfe' (BWV 22), for Quinquagesima Sunday, known as 'Estomihi', from the opening words of the Introit in the Roman Mass: 'Esto mihi in Deum protectorem' – had been performed at St Thomas's on that day before he took office. It was written as a test-piece for his audition before the Council and could obviously not be used again for some time without exciting comment. To add to his normal obligation to provide fifty-nine cantatas for the Sundays and holy days of the year, he was asked to write a cantata – 'Höchsterwünschtes Freudenfest' (BWV 194) – for the dedication of a new organ at Störmthal, near Leipzig, on 2

November 1723. However, we may disregard this work when calculating the total, since it may very well be an adaptation of a lost secular cantata and in any case could be used again for Trinity Sunday in Leipzig. If we deduct from the normal fifty-nine cantatas the nineteen from Weimar and the three Cöthen adaptations, we are still left with thirty-seven cantatas which had to be provided in the first year. Terry, relying on Spitta's dating, reckoned that Bach wrote on an average one cantata a month. Recent research into Bach's handwriting and the watermarks on his paper has shown that many of the cantatas originated much earlier than was previously supposed. Thirty-seven new cantatas works out an average of much nearer three a month, quite apart from the labour of revising and adapting old material. And this ceaseless toil was to be repeated in the next three years, though there are significant gaps in our sources, suggesting either that a good deal has been lost or that Bach was already beginning to repeat earlier material. An indication that he found the burden heavy may be found in the fact that in 1726 he copied out eighteen cantatas by his distant cousin Johann Ludwig Bach, who died five years later. After 1727 his production of cantatas seems to have slackened, as we have seen, though the composition of the *St Matthew Passion* in 1729 is sufficient to show that both his energy and his invention were undiminished. It would appear that his normal weekly duties at the two principal churches aroused his interest less and less. His letter of 1730 to Georg Erdmann, mentioned earlier, reveals considerable dissatisfaction. In 1729 he had taken over the conductorship of the *Collegium musicum* which had previously been directed by the organist of the New Church. This orchestra, consisting mainly of university students, gave weekly concerts at Zimmermann's Coffee House – indoors in the winter and outside in the garden in summer. One would have thought that Bach would have had enough to do without taking on this extra duty. One can only suppose that he found this activity with keen young people more agreeable than his Sunday duties, since he remained in charge of the *Collegium* for at least ten years.

To the casual observer all Bach's church cantatas follow very much the same pattern. There are, however, quite a number of variations in detail, though very little change of style once he had settled in Leipzig. At Mühlhausen, in his early twenties, he had little experience of contemporary music. Unlike Handel, who had become acquainted with opera in Hamburg and was now teaching the Italians how to write Italian music, he had spent most of his early life with the music of the past. As a chorister at Lüneburg (1700–3) he had taken part in a repertory of church music consisting mainly of the works of deceased German composers. The opportunity of hearing secular French and Italian music at Celle was limited, and though he must have performed a good deal of such music while he was a violinist at the court of the Duke of Weimar's brother (1703), his time there was too short for foreign influences of this kind to make any immediate impression on his church music. It is true that his Mühlhausen cantatas show signs of an Italianate style; but it was the style of the past century, not of the new age in which he was growing up. He travelled sixty miles from Lüneburg to hear French music; but when he was organist at Arnstadt (1703–7) he travelled something like 250 miles to Lübeck to hear Buxtehude's organ-playing and church music, and was so entranced by what he heard that he seriously overstayed his leave.

The Mühlhausen cantatas strike one as old-fashioned, as indeed they are; but this does not mean that they are inexpressive. The type of church music that Bach was imitating here was one that was widely current in Europe in the seventeenth century. The composition was more or less continuous, though there might be breaks between sections. Solos and choruses alternated, and the choral writing was either massive and four-square or fugal in texture. If there was an orchestra it would be be used both to accompany the singers and to exchange thematic material with them. English composers of Purcell's time used this kind of structure both in Court odes and in anthems for the Chapel Royal. The only essential difference in Germany was the introduction of chorales. From Bach's Mühlhausen cantatas we may take as an example 'Aus der Tiefe' (Psalm 130). Each section is a setting of one or more verses of the psalm (I quote from the Bible version as it is closer to the German):

TEXT	MUSIC
	Chorus:
1. Out of the depths have I cried unto thee, O Lord.	*Adagio:* Mainly orchestral, but with incidental vocal entries, leading to:

2. Lord, hear my voice; let thine ears be attentive to the voice of my supplications.

Vivace. Homophonic writing, interspersed with brief orchestral passages and leading to:

Bass solo, with oboe obbligato:
Andante. Simultaneously the soprano sings the second verse[1] of the chorale 'Herr Jesu Christ, du höchstes Gut'.

3. If thou, Lord, shouldest mark iniquities, O Lord, who shall stand?

4. But there is forgiveness with thee, that thou mayest be feared.

5. I wait for the Lord,

Chorus:

Adagio: Homophonic, with ornamented interpolations for alto and tenor, leading to:

my soul doth wait, and in his word do I hope.

Largo: Fugal, with decorative accompaniment for oboe and first violin.

Tenor solo:

6. My soul waiteth for the Lord more than they that watch for the morning; I say, more than they that watch for the morning.[3]

[*Andante*]. Simultaneously the alto sings the fifth verse of the same chorale.[2]

---

[1] Erbarm' dich mein in solcher Last,   Pity me as I bear this burden,
  Nimm sie aus meinem Herzen,   Take it from my heart,
Dieweil du sie gebüsset hast   Since thou hast atoned for it
  Am Holz mit Todesschmerzen: On the cross with pains of death:
Auf dass ich nicht mit grossem Weh   That so I may not with great misery
In meinen Sünden untergeh',   Be ruined in my sins,
  Noch ewiglich verzage.   Nor for evermore despair

[2] Und weil ich denn in meinem Sinn,   And since in my mind
  Wie ich zuvor geklaget,   (As I bewailed before)
Auch ein betrübter Sünder bin,   I too am a miserable sinner,
  Den sein Gewissen naget,   Whose conscience gnaws at him,
Und wollte gern in Blute dein   And would gladly in thy blood
Von Sünden abgewaschen sein,   Be washed clean from sin,
  Wie David und Manasse.   Like David and Manasseh.

[3] The German text is slightly different here: 'Meine Seele wartet auf den Herrn von einer Morgenwache bis zu der andern' (My soul waits for the Lord from one morning watch to the next).

Chorus:

7. Let Israel hope in the Lord: for with the Lord there is mercy,

and with him is plenteous redemption.

Adagio, followed by *Un poco allegro* and reverting to *Adagio*. Homophonic, with interchanges between chorus and orchestra, leading to:

Allegro. Short *agitato* passage leading to:

8. And he shall redeem Israel from all his iniquities.

Concluding fugue,[1] with *Adagio* cadence

The structure of this cantata is very different from that of the later cantatas which most people know, where most of the work is occupied by recitatives and *da capo* arias and the chorus is mainly restricted to an opening movement and the final chorale. Here the chorus plays an important and dramatic part in interpreting the text of the psalm, and the solos, extended though they are, are part of an overall scheme rather than independent movements. One notices also that Bach has not yet learned to treat solo instruments as participants in their own right. The oboe obbligato in verse 3 adds considerably to the effectiveness of the bass solo, but the instrument has no introductory ritornello or independent interludes. Bach keeps it on the move but gives it nothing really significant to play: it is decorative rather than melodic. A short extract will illustrate this, and also the first entry of the chorale melody:

EX. 4

[1] An organ arrangement of this fugue (BWV 131a) exists in the handwriting of Johann Christian Kittel (1732–1809), a pupil of Bach's at Leipzig. There is no evidence that it was made by Bach.

In the Weimar cantatas Bach treated the oboe more generously and more sympathetically. For instance, in 'Ich hatte viel Bekümmernis (BWV 21) and 'Weinen, Klagen' (BWV 12), both composed in 1714 and used again in Bach's first year in Leipzig (1723–4), the oboe not only has expressive obbligatos and ritornellos in arias but also has an important solo part in the introductory *sinfonia*. The ritornello to the soprano aria 'Seufzer, Tränen' in 'Ich hatte viel Bekümmernis', already referred to, will illustrate the new enrichment of Bach's imagination, stimulated no doubt by his six years' experience of instrumental music in the Duke's employment. The text of the aria expresses the singer's distress at being separated from God:

EX. 5

Both these cantatas, like others of the same period, may be regarded as transitional works. They include 'operatic' arias and recitatives but the choral writing harks back to an older style – in the opening chorus of 'Ich hatte viel Bekümmernis,' with its repeated cry of 'Ich', and the bold, unsubtle enunciation of 'Das Lamm, das erwürget ist' in the finale;[1] and in the first chorus of 'Weinen, Klagen', where Bach uses a chromatic ground bass which had been the common property of composers for at least seventy years:

EX. 6

(Tears, lamentation, anxiety, fears)

Many years later he remodelled this as the 'Crucifixus' of the B minor Mass, adding four instrumental bars at the beginning (though it is clear from the autograph that the addition was an afterthought).

Evidence that Bach had profited from his acquaintance with

[1] Handel set the same text ('Worthy is the Lamb that was slain') in *Messiah* in much the same way, proceeding, like Bach, to an elaborate fugue at the words 'Blessing and honour, glory and power'. There is no need to suppose that Handel had ever known Bach's cantata: the procedure in both cases derives from an old tradition of choral music. A more interesting comparison is between the fugue subject of the opening chorus in the cantata and the trio 'The flocks shall leave the mountains' in Handel's *Acis and Galatea*. But here again both the theme and its contrapuntal treatment were part of the stock-in-trade of early eighteenth-century composers. There is a further parallel in the first movement of Vivaldi's cello concerto in C minor (Pincherle 434; Malipiero ed., No. 19). The fact that the key is the same in each case makes the coincidence more striking but does not provide any grounds for hasty or improbable conclusions.

French instrumental music is to be found in another Weimar cantata, 'Nun komm, der Heiden Heiland' (BWV 61; BWV 62, with the same title, is a different work, dating from 1724), for the first Sunday in Advent. The opening chorus (a setting of the first verse of Luther's hymn) [1] is in the form of a French overture, consisting of a stately movement in common time, followed by a brisk movement (here marked *gai*) in triple time, with imitative entries, and ending with a short reprise of the first section. In the opening and closing sections the pompous style of the French overture is reserved for the orchestra: the voices merely sing the chorale. In the opening section each voice in turn sings the first line, with the third note sharpened; the second line is sung by all the voices in block harmony. In the middle section the third line is turned into a theme for imitation and considerably extended. All four voices unite to sing the fourth line (which is the same as the first) in the closing section.

Bach also introduced a chorale melody into an opening movement in 'Komm, du süsse Todesstunde' (BWV 161), composed in 1715 for the sixteenth Sunday after Trinity. The elegiac character of the text is explained by reference to the gospel for the day, Luke vii. 11–17, which tells how Jesus raised from the dead the son of the widow of Nain. In death we only sleep till we rise again at the day of resurrection: death then is welcome to the Christian soul. The mood is created from the first by an alto solo accompanied by two recorders:

> Komm, du süsse Todesstunde,
>> Da mein Geist
>> Honig speist
> Aus des Löwen Munde.
> Mache meinen Abschied süsse,
>> Säume nicht,
>> Letztes Licht,
> Dass ich meinen Heiland küsse

('Come, sweet hour of death, while my spirit is fed with honey from the lion's mouth. Make my departure sweet, delay not, my last day, that I may kiss my Saviour.' The reference in lines 2 and 3 is to the story of Samson and the lion's carcass in Judges xiv. 8.)

[1] 'Come, Saviour of the Gentiles, acknowledged child of the Virgin at which all the world wonders: God ordains this birth for him.' The words are a translation of the Ambrosian hymn 'Veni, redemptor gentium', and the melody is adapted from the original plainsong.

Into this gentle song of resignation Bach inserts the melody of the so-called 'Passion Chorale', which is frequently used for Paul Gerhardt's hymn 'O Haupt voll Blut und Wunden' (familiar to English congregations as 'O sacred head surrounded' or 'O sacred head, sore wounded') but also for other hymns. It is not sung but played on a bright solo stop on the organ. Its use here would inevitably suggest the ninth verse of Gerhardt's hymn beginning:

> Wenn ich einmal soll scheiden,
> So scheide nicht von mir.
> Wenn ich den Tod soll leiden,
> So tritt du dann herfür.

> (When my time comes to depart, do not depart from me.
> When I must suffer death, then step forth.)

At the end of the cantata the melody returns again, this time sung by the choir in four-part harmony, to the fourth verse of the chorale 'Herzlich thut mich verlangen'. But not content with presenting the hymn as a congregational offering, Bach adds a counterpoint for the two recorders in unison. There are other examples of this treatment in the Weimar cantatas, and still more in those written at Leipzig. But he never made it a habit; it was merely one way of enriching a familiar tune – a process which could be achieved equally well by the use of new and significant harmony.

One striking example of Bach's adherence to older methods – the cantata 'Christ lag in Todesbanden' (BWV 4) for Easter Day – has already been mentioned: it may now be discussed in more detail. Here Bach was following the example of composers like Buxtehude and Tunder in writing a work which not only uses the complete text of a chorale but introduces the melody (or a variant of it) into every movement. Even the opening *sinfonia* in this cantata alludes to the chorale tune. The successive verses are set as follows:

1. Chorus: simple melody in the soprano.
2. Duet for soprano and alto: variant of the melody.
3. Tenor solo: simple melody with violent counterpoint for the violins.
4. Chorus: melody in the alto, with imitative counterpoint in the other parts.
5. Bass solo: variant, with imitation in the strings.
6. Duet for soprano and tenor: melody divided between the two voices and extended.
7. Chorus: simple four-part setting.

It is obvious that this way of writing a cantata, though it offers opportunities for contrast, is also subject to the danger of monotony, both through the repetition of the tune and also because all the verses are in the same metre. So far as we know, Bach only once again followed the practice of writing an uninterrupted series of variations on a chorale – in the cantata 'Lobe den Herren' (BWV 137) for the twelfth Sunday after Trinity, which dates from 1724 or 1725; and even here the third verse is more a paraphrase than a simple variant of the tune. Elsewhere he sometimes used the unaltered text of a hymn for a cantata and sometimes introduced the melody more than twice. But he evidently realized that a cantata would show more variety and could achieve a genuine, as opposed to an artificial, unity if it were not tied to a single theme.

We now come to the Leipzig cantatas; and the wealth of material here is so great that it is impossible to do more than mention various characteristics and points of interest and illustrate them with selected examples. Choral societies are apt to regard the cantatas as particularly their province. The singers so much enjoy what they have to sing that they hardly notice that in a great many of the works they have relatively little to do. Some statistics will make this clear. Eight of the Leipzig cantatas have no chorus at all. In more than thirty cantatas the chorus merely have to sing a chorale, which is normally at the end. In more than one hundred there is only one chorus in addition to chorales, and in nearly half of these the soprano line is simply a chorale melody, to which the other voices add counterpoints. There seem to be two reasons for this restriction. The first is practical. Bach knew from experience how difficult it was to rehearse his trebles to the point where the weekly performance of the cantatas would be adequate. Hence the less they had to sing the better; and if they merely had to sing a chorale melody in an otherwise elaborate chorus, rehearsal time could be cut to the minimum, since they would know the tune already: all that was necessary was to ensure that they came in at the right time. It is noticeable that in many of these choruses based on a chorale Bach doubles the melody with a slide trumpet or a horn, sometimes described as *corno da tirarsi*, i.e. 'slide horn'. (Since two hands are needed to hold a horn, it cannot very well be fitted with a slide, quite apart from the difficulty, if not the impossi-

32

bility, of incorporating a slide into a conical tube. The problem of this instrument has never been satisfactorily solved.) If the boys could not be heard, at least the tune would be audible, and the support of an instrument might give the singers confidence. The other reason for the restriction of the chorus is probably just as important. Remembering Neumeister's definition of the cantata as 'part of an opera', we can see that the new type of cantata of the early eighteenth century was bound to lay emphasis on the solos. Choruses were rare in early eighteenth-century opera and were employed in the cantata only because there was a choir to sing them and because the chorale was a necessary means of making the congregation feel that they were taking part in the service.

The solos and duets are in fact the chief glory of the cantatas. Though they are 'modern' in treatment, there is one respect in which they hark back to an older tradition, and that is in the occasional use of duets in the form of a dialogue. The practice of writing devotional dialogues was widespread among Protestant German composers in the seventeenth century, such as Andreas Hammerschmidt, one of whose collections, entitled *Dialogi oder Gespräche einer gläubigen Seele mit Gott* (Dialogues or Conversations of a Devout Soul with God), was published in 1645. The dialogue tradition, however, is older than this. It was one of the weapons of the leaders of the Counter-reformation in the sixteenth century, and pieces of this kind were regularly sung at the meetings conducted by St Philip Neri at his Oratory. In one sense it can be traced back further still – to a trope added to the introit for Easter Day in the tenth century, a dialogue between the angel at the tomb and the three Marys which was the starting-point for the so-called liturgical drama of the Middle Ages. Bach actually describes three of his Leipzig cantatas as *dialogi:* 'O Ewigkeit, du Donnerwort' (BWV 60; there is another cantata with the same title (BWV 20), dating from 1724), 1723, 'Ich geh' und suche mit Verlangen' (BWV 49), 1726, and 'Ach Gott, wie manches Herzeleid' (BWV 58), 1727 (for another cantata with the same title (BWV 3) see p. 48). The first of these, for the twenty-fourth Sunday after Trinity, is entitled 'Dialogus zwischen Furcht und Hoffnung' (Dialogue between Fear and Hope). The gospel for the day (Matthew ix. 18–26), like that for the sixteenth Sunday after Trinity, relates a miracle: the raising of Jairus's daughter. The whole cantata, apart from the concluding chorale, is a dialogue between the two allegorical characters, with the addition of one representing the Holy Spirit. Fear sings of the horrors of death, Hope of the comfort and promise of resurrection offered by God. In the opening duet Fear sings the first verse of Johann Rist's hymn 'O Ewigkeit, du Donnerwort' (O eternity, word of thunder), while Hope expresses sublime faith in God: 'Herr, ich warte auf dein Heil' (Lord, I wait for thy salvation). The dialogue is then pursued in a recitative and aria, in which the conflicting ideas of terror and faith continue to be expressed. In a final recitative the Holy Spirit intervenes with an *arioso*, a short passage in strict time similar to an aria in style, patiently repeating the words of Revelation xiv. 13: 'Blessed are the dead which die in the Lord from henceforth',[1] until Fear at last is vanquished.

The characters Fear and Hope appear also in the Easter Monday cantata 'Erfreut euch, ihr Herzen' (BWV 66), 1724(?). Here the doubts expressed about Christ's resurrection are resolved in a single lengthy recitative, including an extended arioso in which two contrary points of view are expressed by means of imitation:

EX. 7

(Hope: My eye sees the risen saviour . . .
Fear: No eye sees the risen saviour . . .)

[1] This text was set by Brahms in the final chorus of *Ein deutsches Requiem*.

The two singers then unite in a duet in which both confess their faith in God. These are not, however, the original words for which the music was written. Bach has here borrowed from a secular cantata written for the birthday of Prince Leopold of Anhalt-Cöthen in December 1718: 'Der Himmel dacht' auf Anhalts Ruhm und Glück' (BWV 66a). Though the music of this work is lost, the libretto was printed, and though it is longer than the text of the Easter cantata the correspondences are unmistakable. Here too we have a dialogue cantata: the characters are Glückseligkeit (Happiness) and Fama (Fame), who finally unite to sing the praises of the Prince.

Bach had used the dialogue form in his Mühlhausen cantata 'Gottes Zeit' (BWV 106), where the alto sings the text of Psalm xxxi. 6:[1] 'Into thy hands I commend my spirit: for thou hast redeemed me, O Lord thou God of truth', and the bass has Jesus's reply to the penitent thief (Luke xxiii, 43): 'Today shalt thou be with me in paradise.' The two texts, however, are not sung simultaneously; but when the bass solo is well advanced the alto enters with the chorale 'Mit Fried' und Freud' ich fahr' dahin' (With peace and joy I go hence), just as in 'O Ewigkeit, du Donnerwort' the alto sings the chorale above the tenor solo. In terms of musical technique there is no difference between this and other arias in which a chorale is introduced (as in 'Aus der Tiefe'). The only difference is in the close association between the two singers; though one is singing a chorale they are still engaged in dialogue. This is equally true of 'Ich geh' und suche mit Verlangen', mentioned above (p. 33), where in the final duet, the soprano sings the seventh verse of Nicolai's hymn 'Wie schön leuchtet der Morgenstern' to its proper melody, while the bass, representing Christ as the bridegroom, speaks of his love and announces his coming. The extract on the next page (Ex. 8) shows the two melodies in combination: it will be noticed that the bass sings a varied form of the hymn-tune.

The image of Christ as the heavenly bridegroom appears also in the two superb duets in one of Bach's best-known works, the cantata 'Wachet auf' (BWV 140), 1731, for the twenty-seventh Sunday after Trinity. Here the whole cantata is based on the parable of the ten virgins, as related in the gospel for the day (Matthew xxv. 1-13), with its dramatic climax: 'And at mid-

[1] Verse 5 in the Bible version.

EX. 8

(*Soprano:* How heartfelt is my joy [that my treasure is alpha and omega, the beginning and the end]
Bass: I have always loved thee, [and therefore I draw thee to me][1]

[1] A reference to Jeremiah xxxi. 3: 'Yea, I have loved thee with an everlasting love: therefore with loving-kindness have I drawn thee.'

36

night there was a cry made, Behold the bridegroom cometh; go
ye out to meet him' (v. 6). In the first duet – slow and passionate
with an elaborate obbligato for the *violino piccolo* (a small-sized
violin, tuned a minor third higher than the normal instrument) –
the Christian soul expresses a fervent desire for the saviour
('Wann kommst du, mein Heil?'), in a phrase identical with the
opening of the alto solo 'Erbarme dich, mein Gott' in the *St
Matthew Passion*, while Jesus answers with the assurance that
he is here. In the second duet all anxiety has been resolved. The
company has come in to the wedding feast, and soul and bridegroom are united in one of Bach's happiest inventions:

EX. 9

(*Soprano:* My friend is mine.
Bass: And I am thine.
Both: Nothing shall separate our love.)

In subtlety of invention the most remarkable of Bach's dialogues is to be found in the Whit Sunday cantata 'Erschallet, ihr
Lieder' (BWV 172), originally composed at Weimar and revived

in his first year at Leipzig. Here we have a duet in which the Soul appeals to the Holy Spirit to come ('Komm, lass mich nicht länger warten, komm, du sanfter Himmelswind'), while the Spirit brings refreshment ('Ich erquicke dich, mein Kind'). The two voices are closely interwoven, and the bass – an *ostinato* at different levels – is strongly independent. But as if this was not enough, an instrumental counterpoint is added in the shape of a richly decorated version of the chorale melody 'Komm, heiliger Geist', played in one version by the organ and in another by the *oboe d'amore* (a mezzo-soprano oboe, pitched a minor third lower than the normal instrument). The whole movement is uniquely appropriate to the festival. Considering the effectiveness of the dialogue form, it is curious that Bach wrote so few. There are none in the church cantatas after 'Wachet auf'. In fact they occur in only twelve works altogether – one at Mühlhausen, three at Weimar, and eight at Leipzig. Though the duet 'Herr, dein Mitleid' in Part III of the *Christmas Oratorio* is adapted from a dialogue for Hercules and Virtue in 'Lasst uns sorgen' (BWV 213), in which kisses are exchanged *ad nauseam*, in the adaptation both singers are given the same words.

Bach's singers were never of the calibre of the international soloists who sang in opera all over Europe. It is unlikely that Handel would have looked twice at the nineteen-year-old tenor whom Bach accepted for the choir in 1729. But the evidence of the solos written for them makes it clear that the best pupils of the Thomasschule must have had at least a very competent technique. A bass who can negotiate this passage from the opening movement of 'Es ist euch gut, dass ich hingehe' (BWV 108):

EX. 10

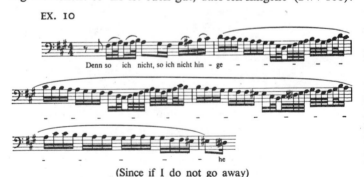

(Since if I do not go away)

not only needs good lungs but must also have acquired the kind of agility that present-day singers are rarely called upon to master. Quality of tone is a different matter: and here we may guess that if we had been present when the cantatas were first performed we might not always have experienced rapture. Ears which are accustomed to hearing alto solos sung by a female contralto or mezzo-soprano might find it difficult to accommodate themselves to the tone of a boy who was too old to be a soprano and too young to be a baritone.

It is evident that Bach, like the opera composers of his time, learned much from the practice of instrumental music. This is not to say that his vocal writing is instrumental in character: that term has too often been applied to music of the past which is elaborate. The influence of instrumental music is to be seen rather in the springy rhythms which are characteristic of the dance or a concerto movement, and in the use of expressive contours which in fact often sound better on the violin or oboe than they do when sung. Hence it often happens that the introduction to an aria sounds as if we were going to hear a movement from a purely instrumental work, until the voice enters with the same material and turns the piece into a song. In an aria like the following, from 'Gott fähret auf mit Jauchzen' (BWV 43), the voice dances as convincingly as the instrumental introduction which precedes it:

EX. 11

(Yes, a thousand times a thousand accompany the chariot
to sing the praises of the King of kings)

Or consider the following, from 'Ich bin vergnügt mit meinem Glücke' (BWV 84), where the rhythm is equally persuasive:

EX. 12

39

(I eat with joy my scanty bread and with all my heart do
not grudge my neighbour his)

Voice and instrument are closely linked, and the link becomes
even stronger when Bach adopts the practice, common in
eighteenth-century opera, of interrupting the voice with an
instrumental ritornello after the first statement and then starting
again with the same phrase and continuing without a break.[1]
It must be admitted, however, that there are occasions – and
they are not infrequent – when he seems to have thought of the
instrumental melody first, without bothering overmuch about
the words, and then fitted them in as best he could. The melody
of this aria from the funeral ode for Queen Christine (BWV 198)
is charming, but no one can pretend that it is an ideal vehicle for
the text:

EX. 13

(How cheerfully did the noble lady die)

Apart from superficial details of structure, such as the treatment of instrumental ritornelli and the use of the *da capo* form
(where Bach was sometimes content to stop the repetition at the
end of the introduction), it is impossible to discern any general
plan which is followed in the arias. What is common to all of
them is his extraordinary capacity for developing even the simplest material into a coherent work of art. The ability to go on is
something that all composers have to acquire; Bach seems to
have possessed it by instinct once he had served his apprenticeship.
A favourite device is to lead the music into a related key, once
the voice is well under way, either by extending the initial phrase
or by employing sequence. A simple example of such extension

[1] Familiar examples are the soprano aria 'Ich folge dir gleichfalls' from
the *St John Passion*, the bass aria 'Mache dich, mein Herze, rein' from the
St Matthew Passion, and 'Mein gläubiges Herze' (known in England as
'My heart ever faithful') from 'Also hat Gott die Welt geliebt' (BWV 68).

is the alto aria from 'Gott, der Herr, ist Sonn' und Schild' (BWV 79), written for the Reformation festival in 1725:

EX. 14

(God is our sun and shield. Therefore our thankful hearts praise his goodness, which he cherishes for his little flock)

Here the music grows imperceptibly from the first two bars and by an effortless process ends in the key of A major. The sequence in bars 5–8 seems so inevitable that one hardly notices it. In the tenor aria from 'Herr, gehe nicht ins Gericht' (BWV 105) it is more obvious, but the modulation proceeds as smoothly as in the previous example:

EX. 15

(If I can only make Jesus my friend, Mammon means nothing to me)

But this is only a fragment of Bach's invention: to do it full justice one would have to quote the whole of this splendid aria, complete with the horn part and the brilliant demisemiquavers for the first violins.

This art of construction is exempt from any danger of monotony by the imaginative contours of the melodic line and a constant freedom of rhythm. It is rare in Bach to find anything as symmetrical as this aria[1] from 'Nimm, was dein ist, und gehe hin' (BWV 144):

EX. 16

(Do not murmur, dear Christian, when something does not happen as you would wish)

More often a twist is given to the phrase lengths to avoid too much regularity. This may happen even in the simplest song tune, as in Miecke's first aria in 'Mer hahn en neue Oberkeet' (BWV 212), known as the *Peasant Cantata*:

EX. 17

(Yes, but it can be too much of a good thing when a couple get really friendly)

where the repetition of the second bar not merely extends the four-bar phrase but adds to the charm of the melody. Where the text is plaintive, Bach may break up the melodic line to suggest the cramping force of grief, as in 'Ach, mein Sinn' or 'Es ist vollbracht' in the *St John Passion*, or perhaps most vividly in the aria in 'Lobet Gott in seinen Reichen' (BWV 11), known as the *Ascension Oratorio*, where the Christian expresses dismay that Jesus is leaving the earth and begs him to stay:

[1] Schweitzer (*J. S. Bach*, English ed. [1911], ii, p. 200, n. 2) was worried about the declamation in this aria and felt certain that the music was originally written for a different text. In view of Bach's other adaptations this may very well be true; on the other hand his setting of words was not invariably faultless, as Ex. 13 shows.

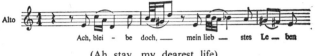

(Ah stay, my dearest life)

When Bach was completing the B minor Mass some years later he remodelled and shortened this aria to form the 'Agnus Dei', for which the appealing character of the music is very appropriate.

The influence of the opera aria is never far away in Bach's cantatas. Sometimes it finds expression in bold, unsubtle strokes, as in the pompous aria, with trumpet obbligato, in which Fame praises the charms of the Queen of Poland in 'Tönet, ihr Pauken' (BWV 214):

EX. 19

(Crown and glory of crowned ladies, Queen, with your name I fill
the circle of the globe)

The image of a baroque Dr Bartolo seems to lurk behind these assertive strains. There could be no better demonstration of the link between sacred and secular than the fact that Bach used this aria in Part I of the *Christmas Oratorio* to sing the praises of God come down to earth:

> Grosser Herr, o starker König,
> Liebster Heiland, o wie wenig
> Achtest du der Erden Pracht.

(Great Lord, powerful King, beloved Saviour, how little regard
hast thou for earthly pomp.)

He was forgetting, however, that he was not celebrating earthly pomp but the poverty of Christ in the manger. The contrast between the two texts is most noticeable in the middle section of the aria:

'Tönet, ihr Pauken':

> Was der Tugend stets gefällt
> Und was nur Heldinnen haben,
> Sein dir angeborne Gaben.

(You have as inborn gifts what always pleases Virtue and what only noble ladies possess.)

Christmas Oratorio:

> Der die ganze Welt erhält,
> Ihre Pracht und Zier erschaffen,
> Muss in harten Krippen schlafen.

(He who upholds the whole world and has created its splendour and its glory must sleep in a rough manger.)

Terry was aware of the conflict but misunderstood its significance:

Is it possible to misread the inspiration of this masculine music? Not the lowliness of Bethlehem, but the celestial might of the Lord of heaven is Bach's theme. How proudly it is declaimed! How brilliantly the trumpet echoes through the royal halls! Not even with her proud Habsburg traditions could Maria Josepha have inspired this virile music![1]

Unfortunately there is no question of inspiration here. The music, like most of Bach's, was written to order: what resulted was the product of his inexhaustible invention. He may or may not have had a regard for the daughter of the late Emperor Joseph I, but he knew very well the sort of music that was proper for a queen's birthday.

Arias reflecting the pleasures of rural life are not uncommon in eighteenth-century opera. In Bach's cantatas, though he quite often uses the characteristic 12/8 rhythm (for instance, in the funeral ode for Queen Christine, cited above), there are only three arias which can strictly be called pastoral, and all of them occur, naturally enough, in cantatas on the subject of the Good Shepherd: 'Du Hirte Israel, höre' (BWV 104), 1724, 'Ich bin ein guter Hirt' (BWV 85), 1725, and 'Er rufet seinen Schafen mit Namen' (BWV 175). The first two of these cantatas are for the second Sunday after Easter, known as 'Misericordia Domini', from the opening words of the Introit for the day in the Roman Mass: 'Misericordia Domini plena est terra'. Their sub-

[1] Quoted by Whittaker, op. cit., ii, p. 651.

44

ject is closely related to the gospel for the day (John x. 11–16). In the second of them the tenor sings, to a gently rocking rhythm, of Christ's love in tending his sheep ('Seht, was die Liebe tut'). In the first the soloist congratulates the happy flock on the joy that is theirs. The harmony is such an essential element in the creation of atmosphere that the accompaniment must be quoted as well as the tune:

EX. 20

(Happy flock, Jesus's sheep, the world is for you a heavenly kingdom)

If we are looking for signs of rustic jollity we need not go further than the bass aria in 'Liebster Gott, wann werd' ich sterben' (BWV 8), which might equally well be an adaptation from yet another 'peasant cantata' or a movement from an instrumental suite:

EX. 21

(Away, you senseless, futile worries)

The text continues: 'Mich rufet mein Jesus: wer sollte nicht gehn?' (My Jesus calls me: who would not go?). The cantata,

45

like 'Komm, du süsse Todesstunde', is concerned with death and resurrection. In the opening movement the chorale which gives its name to the work is sung against a background of tolling bells (flute and pizzicato violins and violas), while the oboes play a doleful duet. In the second movement the tenor urges his soul not to be terrified at his last hour, while the bells still toll in the bass. In the recitative which follows, the alto cries out in anguish at the thought of death. It is at this point that the bass aria quoted above is introduced and immediately blows all the clouds away with its jigging dance.

Finally the close connection which also exists between the operatic aria and the solo concerto may be illustrated by the opening movement, very Italianate in style, of 'Leichgesinnte Flattergeister' (BWV 181), a cantata for Sexagesima Sunday, dating from 1724:

EX. 22

(Frivolous and flighty people rob themselves of the strength of the word)

The words refer to the gospel for the day (Luke viii. 5–15) – the parable of the sower – and particularly to verse 12: 'Those by the way-side are they that hear: then cometh the devil, and taketh away the word out of their hearts, lest they should believe and be saved.' Earnest commentators have laboured to assure us that the music represents 'the fluttering of the evil harpies and the flapping of their wings', as well as 'the nervous, eager movements of the hungry seekers after seeds'.[1] Needless to say, no one hearing the music without knowing the subject would have the remotest idea that this was Bach's intention; nor is a knowledge of the subject essential to appreciate the way it is treated, any more than one need know the story of *Till Eulenspiegel* in order to enjoy Strauss's music. If the words were Italian, the aria would be perfectly acceptable in an opera, particularly as the feminine endings are very characteristic of Italian libretti. If there were no words at all, we should listen to it quite happily as the first movement of a concerto, with a solo bassoon or cello to replace the voice.

In terms of quantity, as we have seen, the choruses play only a minor role in the cantatas; but no one would dream of suggesting that they are unimportant. Abundant as Bach's invention is, it is never more remarkable than when he is building a choral movement round a familiar chorale, whether he is making the chorus sing in unison against an orchestral concerto, as in the fifth section of 'Ein feste Burg' (BWV 80), or, as so frequently happens, uniting both orchestra and the altos, tenors and basses in a complex figuration through which the sopranos, generally reinforced by an instrument, continue to declaim the lines of the chorale. Though he abandoned quite early the idea of building a cantata entirely on the verses of a chorale, employing the same melody for each, he sometimes used a complete chorale text without adhering consistently to the melody, and still more often paraphrased the verses or interspersed them with recitatives and independent arias. In the latter case the chorale melody may be heard in the course of the work as well as at the beginning and end, either set for chorus, or given to a soloist, or played on an instrument. 'Ein feste Burg' is a good example of this intermittent use of a chorale melody. The chorus which was mentioned just now occurs in the body of the work. At the end is a simple statement of the chorale in four-part harmony. At the beginning is a tremendous polyphonic structure, with the chorale played in canon by trumpet and oboes on the one hand and the basses of the orchestra on the other, and an elaborate piece of

[1] Whittaker, op. cit. i. p. 713.

47

imitative choral writing which also derives its thematic material from the chorale. This is followed by a duet in which the soprano sings an ornamented version of the chorale against a furious background for violins and violas, while the bass soloist has a florid counterpoint. After an independent recitative and aria comes the unison chorus, followed by an independent duet. The simple chorale rounds off the cantata. Often the chorale plays a less important part than it does here. In 'Wachet auf' (BWV 140), for instance, it occurs only three times: in the opening chorus, as a tenor solo with a dance-like accompaniment, and in a four-part setting at the end. (The idea seems to be widespread that the tenor solo should be sung by all the tenors, but there is no justification for this in the score.) The other four movements are independent recitatives and duets.

These examples, and others like them, do not exhaust the possible ways of treating a chorale. The incorporation of the melody into a French overture in the Weimar cantata 'Nun komm, der Heiden Heiland' (BWV 61) has already been mentioned (see p. 30). In 'Gott, der Herr, ist Sonn' und Schild' (BWV 79) the familiar chorale 'Nun danket alle Gott' (Now thank we all our God) is set in four-part harmony against a jubilant march which has already been heard in the opening chorus. It would be more difficult to imagine a more stirring way of celebrating the Reformation Festival: the faithful Protestants are marching shoulder to shoulder. In some cantatas the influence of the chorale is so pervasive that it makes its appearance even in recitative – either in the form of interpolations by soloists, as in 'Ich hab in Gottes Herz und Sinn' (BWV 92), or as a result of the intervention of the chorus, as in 'Ach Gott, wie manches Herzeleid' (BWV 3). [1] Even when the chorale melody itself is not quoted Bach sometimes alludes to it in the opening notes of an aria. Perhaps the most remarkable example of choral intervention in a recitative is to be found in the Weimar cantata 'Gleich wie der Regen und Schnee vom Himmel fällt' (BWV 18), where the chorus enters with extracts from the Litany. The recitative, which is accompanied by strings, is more *arioso* than

[1] It is possible, though unlikely, that the chorale in this example was meant to be sung by the four soloists, all of whom are involved in the recitative. For another cantata with the same title (BWV 58), described as 'Concerto in dialogo', see p. 33.

recitative: it is shared between the tenor and bass soloists and demands considerable virtuosity from both, particularly the tenor. The text of the opening will illustrate the unusual structure of this movement:

Tenor solo:
>Mein Gott, hier wird mein Herze sein:
>Ich öffne dir's in meines Jesu Namen;
>>So streue deinen Samen
>>Als in ein gutes Land hinein.
>Mein Gott, hier wird mein Herze sein;
>Lass solches Frucht und hundertfältig bringen.
>O Herr, Herr, hilf! o Herr, lass wohlgelingen.

Chorus (soprano):
>Du wollest deinen Geist und Kraft zum Worte geben.

Chorus (tutti):
>Erhör uns, lieber Herre Gott!

(My God, here will my heart be: I open it to theee in Jesus' name; so sow thy seed on me as on a good soil. My God, here will my heart be; let it bring forth fruit a hundredfold. O Lord, help me! O Lord, grant that I may prosper.
>Thou wilt give thy spirit and strength to the word.
>Hear us, good lord.

The reference in the recitative, as in 'Leichtgesinnte Flattergeister' (see p. 46), is to the parable of the sower. Both the words and the music of the chorus are borrowed from the Lutheran liturgy, where one choir intones the intercessions of the Litany, while the other responds, as here, in four-part harmony.

There is no doubt that the practice of building a chorus on a chorale was both a challenge and a stimulus to Bach's invention; it continues a long-standing tradition of church music and it offers an instructive parallel to his organ preludes on hymn tunes. But he could be equally resourceful without this framework. In 'Preise, Jerusalem, den Herrn' (BWV 119), written for the election of the Leipzig town council in 1723, he again constructs the opening chorus in the form of a French overture, only this time without incorporating a chorale. In this magnificent movement, scored for four trumpets, timpani, two recorders,[1] three oboes, strings and organ, the voices are heard only in the middle section in 12/8 time; the stately introduction and coda are reserved for

[1] The recorders have very little chance of being heard, which is probably the reason why for most of the time they are in unison with the first oboe; but they come into their own later in the work.

the orchestra. The choral writing here (and also in the final chorus) is so elaborate that it must have needed more than the usual amount of rehearsal: one cannot help wondering whether on a festal occasion of this kind Bach enlisted the help of university students to augment the normal choir. This introductory chorus is an outstanding example of the close relationship between his orchestral music and his choral works. Even more remarkable is the opening chorus of the Christmas cantata 'Unser Mund sei voll Lachens' (BWV 110), where he borrowed the overture of his Suite No. 4 in D major for orchestra (BWV 1069), adding two flutes to the score (though without any independent parts) and making minor modifications. Here again the chorus sings only in the middle section in 9/8 time. In arranging the opening of this section Bach cut out the first bar of the original; but as the omission of a bar would have upset the proportions he inserted an extra bar after the fourth bar of the orchestral version, so that by the fifth bar the two versions correspond. It is a tribute to his technical skill that no one hearing the cantata without knowing the Suite would guess that this tinkering had taken place.

The choruses which have been mentioned so far are brilliant and festal. There are others which are penitential in character, such as the opening chorus of 'Schauet doch und sehet' (BWV 46), which later became the 'Qui tollis' of the B minor Mass, or the first movement of 'Herr, gehe nicht ins Gericht' (BWV 105), from which the tenor aria was quoted earlier (see Ex. 15). The opening chorus of 'Herr, gehe nicht' is divided into two sections, the first slow and the second brisk. The whole of the first section, lasting for forty-seven bars, is a setting of the first half of Psalm cxliii. 2: '[Lord], enter not into judgment with thy servant' – an allusion to the parable of the unjust steward (Luke xvi. 1–9). Throughout this section the basses of the orchestra maintain a ponderous, plodding motion, which continues virtually without a break until they finally come to rest on a dominant pedal (i.e. D in the key of G minor). Above this the upper instruments seem to plead for mercy; before they have finished their introduction the voices enter with broken cries. In all Bach's cantatas it would be hard to find a more vivid portrayal of the terrors of judgment. Nor is this all that is remarkable in this work. It ends with a unique setting of the closing chorale, in which an agitated semiquaver trembling on the strings gradually subsides, the movement changing first into triplets and then into single quavers; and after the voices have sung their final lines:

> Dass auf dieser weiten Erden
> Keiner soll verloren werden,
> Sondern ewig leben soll,
> Wenn er nur ist glaubensvoll,

([I know] that on this wide earth none shall be lost, but he shall live for ever, if only he has faith.)

the basses of the orchestra and the organ are silent and the movement ends plaintively with the upper strings.

While it is true that the majority of Bach's choruses are set in a style which allows for considerable elaboration, there are one or two in a more austere style which seems to look back to an older form of polyphony, such as the opening chorus of 'Ach Gott vom Himmel sieh' darein' (BWV 2), built round the chorale melody which Mozart used for the two armed men in *Die Zauberflöte*, or the first chorus of 'Nimm, was dein ist, und gehe hin' (BWV 144), which is virtually a motet with the instruments doubling the voices throughout. Though Bach in his later days was thought to be old-fashioned, this could hardly have been said of him in 1724, when 'Nimm, was dein ist' was written. His occasional reversion to an older style must be seen as the sign of respect which every genuine composer has for the work of those who have preceded him. There are parallels in the work of Monteverdi and Purcell, both of whom not only wrote in an up-to-date idiom but also showed their mastery of sixteenth-century polyphony.

Bach, like many of his contemporaries, regularly used the word 'concerto' to describe a cantata. The term was not casually applied: it meant that the work was not merely a vocal composition but something to be performed by an ensemble of voices and instruments. Performance of the cantatas with nothing more than an organ accompaniment must be regarded only as a makeshift, to be tolerated, if at all, when the requisite instrumentalists are lacking. Bach's orchestra did not provide a mere accompaniment to the singers, except in the relatively few cases where the instruments simply double the voices. Both in choruses and in solos the instruments have a vital part to play in the ensemble. An aria with violin obbligato is not simply a vehicle for the singer's artistry and skill: it is a duet for voice and instrument, in which the instrument very often has the more demanding part. The scores of Bach's cantatas show that the instruments in each case were carefully chosen. The choice was naturally limited, and there may well have been occasions when he had to forego the use of a particular instrument because there was no player available. He was adaptable up to a point and willing to modify the instrumentation, if necessary, when revising a work for a later performance. But in general it would appear that he was acutely aware of the tone of instruments and knew exactly where he wanted them. The provision of the necessary instruments is no longer a difficulty at the present day, when professional players of the recorder, lute and bass viol are readily available. But the problem of balance, particularly in choruses, is sometimes so serious that one wonders whether Bach himself always realized the difficulty. A small choir, which in any case is essential for these works, will not drown the orchestra; but the texture of four vocal parts may easily make it difficult to hear clearly the more delicate instruments. In the opening chorus of 'Schauet doch' the elaborate counterpoints for the two recorders are not easily heard above the voices and the strings, which may be the reason why Bach transferred the parts to flutes when he adapted the music for the 'Qui tollis' in the B minor Mass. The trumpets have no difficulty in dominating the orchestra in the first chorus of the *Christmas Oratorio*, but the two flutes have a much harder task to make their independent line audible in the middle section. How, one may ask, is a conductor to ensure that the oboes are clearly heard throughout the first chorus of 'O ewiges Feuer' (BWV 34)? And here it may be added that the legend that the oboe of Bach's time was a coarse instrument has no foundation. Bach often doubled his instruments, but even this is not always sufficient to produce a just balance, particularly when he is ringing the changes on trumpets, wood-wind and strings. It would seem that in such cases he was prepared to accept a compromise and rely on the effect produced by an overall activity.

Bach wrote obbligatos for every instrument in the orchestra except the trombone (which was almost entirely restricted to doubling the voices in chorales)[1] and the double bass, with the addition of extra instruments such as the *violino piccolo*, the *viola d'amore* (an instrument with six or seven

[1] One exception is 'O Jesu Christ, mein's Lebens Licht' (BWV 118), where the trombones form part of a wind ensemble; but this is funeral music for

strings played with the bow and a number of subsidiary wire strings which vibrate in sympathy), the *violoncello piccolo* (a small-sized cello, useful for playing in the higher register), and the bass viol, described simply as *viola da gamba* (leg viol), which is actually the generic name for all the viol family; the bass was the only one in normal use in Bach's time. There is only one solo for the viola[1]. He must have had an unusually competent bassoon-player at Weimar since there is a very elaborate obbligato for the instrument in the alto and tenor duet in 'Mein Gott, wie lang', ach lange' (BWV 155): he wrote nothing as difficult as this at Leipzig. In fact, it is only rarely that the bassoon has a solo part: most of the time it is simply doubling the bass, whether it is marked in the score or not. The choice of solo instruments depended on the character of the music. Flute, oboe and violin would obviously be equally suitable for sad and merry arias: the selection of one rather than the others would depend on the key, on the voice or voices that were singing, and on the need for variety in the cantata as a whole. The horn[2] was an obvious choice for hunting arias, but there is no place for these in the church cantatas, except in 'Siehe, ich will Fischer aussenden' (BWV 88), where, since the gospel relates the miraculous draught of fishes, the bass solo takes its text from Jeremiah xvi. 16:

> Behold, I will send for many fishers, saith the Lord, and they shall fish them; and after will I send for many hunters, and they shall hunt them from every mountain, and from every hill, and out of the holes of the rocks.

---

the open air, nor is it strictly a cantata. The other – and a remarkable one – is the first movement of 'Es ist nichts Gesundes an meinem Leibe' (BWV 25), where a wind ensemble including three trombones is heard playing the Passion chorale against an independent contrapuntal texture for the voices.

[1] In 'Wo soll ich fliehen hin' (BWV 5). The solo in 'Herr Gott, dich loben wir' (BWV 16), marked *violetta*, is an alternative for the *oboe da caccia* (alto oboe). *Violetta* was a common name for the viola in the eighteenth century, though it occurs in only three works by Bach. Terry's theory (*Bach's Orchestra* [London, 1932], pp. 127–8) that it was a different instrument from the viola can hardly be supported. There is no separate part for it in the secular cantata 'Preise dein Glücke' (BWV 215), where it is marked in the score in unison with the violins in the alto aria.

[2] *Corno* or *corno da caccia* (hunting horn). Terry's attempt to distinguish between these two instruments (*Bach's Orchestra*, pp. 44–7) has no validity.

Here it is natural that two horns would be added to the orchestra in the second part of the aria. The instrument is also suitable for battle pieces, for instance the soprano aria 'Unsre Stärke heisst zu schwach' in 'Wär' Gott nicht mit uns diese Zeit' (BWV 14); but it is a little puzzling to find a horn taking part in the opening chorus of 'Erforsche mich, Gott' (BWV 136), since the words, taken from Psalm cxxxix. 23, hardly suggest horn calls: 'Try me, O God, and seek the ground of my heart; prove me and examine my thoughts'. Perhaps Bach thought so himself: at any rate when he adapted the chorus for the 'In gloria Dei Patris' of the A major Mass (BWV 234) he left out the horn. Whittaker[1] may be right in suggesting that the music of this chorus was originally a setting of entirely different words. Elsewhere the horn is appropriate to any movement of a festal and happy character. The same is true of the trumpet, which in eighteenth-century opera is regularly associated with heroic arias.

When Bach employs wind instruments in groups he generally uses three trumpets, two horns,[2] two flutes or recorders, and two or three oboes, one of which might be an alto (*oboe da caccia*), or alternatively there might be two *oboi da caccia* or two *oboi d'amore*. The only instance in Bach's works of two bassoons is in the 'Quoniam tu solus' of the B minor Mass. Four trumpets are found in two cantatas (BWV 63 and 119), both festal works, and three horns in only one (BWV 143): presumably Bach used the extra resources on these occasions simply because they happened to be available. In three cases he wrote for three recorders: in an aria in 'Es ist nichts Gesundes an meinem Leibe' (BWV 25), in a recitative in 'Das neugebor'ne Kindelein' (BWV 122), and in the introductory recitative and aria of 'Er rufet seinen Schafen mit Namen' (BWV 175), where they very happily evoke the pastoral atmosphere suggested by the words.[3] There is also a unique example of three flutes used as obbligato instruments in the secular cantata 'Schleicht, spielende Wellen, und murmelt

[1] Op. cit., i, p. 349.

[2] Trumpets and horns are used together only once, in the *dramma per musica* 'Zerreisset, zersprenget, zertrümmert die Gruft' (BWV 205) – an indication that normally the horns were played by trumpeters.

[3] The reference in the recitative is to verse 3 of the gospel for the day (John x. 1–10): 'He calleth his own sheep by name, and leadeth them out.'

gelinde' (BWV 206), written for the birthday of the King of Poland, where the River Pleisse sings:

> Hört doch! der sanften Flöten Chor
> Erfreut die Brust, ergötzt das Ohr.

(But hark! the gentle chorus of flutes gladdens the heart and delights the ear.)

In all this music a keyboard instrument has a part to play – an unassuming part in general but an essential one, not least when the accompaniment to an aria consists merely of a figured bass. This background of harmony is absent only on the infrequent occasions when the accompaniment is reserved for treble instruments or where there is a specific indication that it is not required, as in the tenor aria:

> Ach, schlage doch bald, sel'ge Stunde,
> Den allerletzten Glockenschlag

(Ah, blessed hour, strike soon the final peal.)

from 'Christus, der ist mein Leben' (BWV 95), where the pizzicato accompaniment of the strings is self-sufficient. The keyboard instrument is part of the *continuo*, which normally includes also the cellos, double basses and bassoon. In secular cantatas it was the harpsichord, whether performances were in the open air or indoors; in church cantatas it was the organ. Terry[1] tried hard to prove that the harpsichord was also used in church music, but the evidence is far from conclusive. It is true that when Bach was asked in 1724 to perform his Passion music in St Nicholas's Church one of his objections was that the harpsichord needed repairing; but this does not necessarily mean that he required it for the performance. It is significant that in all the movements which have a written out obbligato part for a keyboard instrument – there are several – they are specifically intended for the organ. When Bach adapted the first movement of his harpsichord concerto in D minor (BWV 1052a)[2] for the cantata 'Wir müssen durch viel Trübsal in das Reich Gottes eingehen' (BWV 146) he rewrote the keyboard solo part an octave lower for the organ. By contrast, in the *Coffee Cantata* ('Schweigt stille, plaudert nicht', BWV 211) there is an obbligato part marked

[1] *Bach's Orchestra*, p. 164.
[2] Or the lost violin concerto from which the harpsichord concerto was derived.

55

cembalo (harpsichord). The harpsichord may have been needed for rehearsals of the church cantatas (e.g. the figured harpsichord part in the alto aria in 'Mein liebster Jesus ist verloren', BWV 154, which cannot have been intended for use in performance), and may in emergencies, such as occur in most churches, have replaced the organ; but there is nothing to show that it was in regular use.

Much ink has been spilt on the subject of Bach's alleged 'symbolism'. 'Motives' have been catalogued, and we are asked to notice how this or that detail of the words is reflected in the music. Few supporters of this doctrine, however, have bothered to study eighteenth-century music as a whole. If they had, they would have realized that it was an accepted principle of the period that music should 'paint the passions', i.e. that each piece should represent a definite emotion. Where vocal music is concerned, this is not difficult, except where the middle section of a *da capo* aria has an entirely different mood. Eighteenth-century theorists discussed this question at some length, in the same way that their contemporaries in the field of literature discussed the treatment of 'topics' in rhetoric. But when Mattheson and others talked about the way in which varying emotions could be represented in music – the so-called *Affekten-Lehre* – they were not primarily concerned with analysing the works of their contemporaries: their purpose was to instruct composers who were inexperienced. Their teaching, to put it at its lowest, was aimed at suggesting a series of clichés which would fit a variety of situations. Anyone who considers the actual music of the period must be struck by the fact that though a large number of formulas are common to all composers the way in which they are used varies considerably.

The same is true of tonality. We might be inclined to believe that the minor key represents sadness and the major gaiety. But there are examples of love-songs in the minor and laments in the major. At a later period Schubert showed unmistakably how poignant the change from minor to major could be. Bach also knew the emotional force of a major tonality. In the *St Matthew Passion*, after Judas has repented and cast down the pieces of silver, there is an aria in which the singer pleads for the release of Jesus:

Gebt mir meinen Jesum wieder!
Seht, das Geld, den Mörderlohn,
Wirft euch der verlorne Sohn
Zu den Füssen nieder.

(Give me back my Jesus! See, the prodigal casts down the money, the
murderer's reward, at your feet.)

The music is in G major, and there is a florid obbligato for solo
violin. The melody seems to be suave and gentle: at a first
acquaintance we might not find it appropriate. It is only when
we come to know the piece better that we realize that it is not
Judas who is appealing but ourselves, and in terms that are
meant to melt a stubborn heart. This is how children ask for
something they want desperately, even if they know it is impossible. The major key is not a denial of pathos: it is the ideal
language for it.

It is idle, therefore, to expect that the clue to Bach's means of
expression will always lie on the surface. There are, however,
many places where the relation between the music and the mood
of the words is obvious enough, and here he is doing no more
than his contemporaries did, whether in opera or in oratorio. It
was also quite natural, and quite in accord with the æsthetic of
the time, that the character of the music – its rhythms, its melodic contours, its harmonies – might be suggested more by individual words than by the text as a whole. Nor is this merely an
eighteenth-century conception: all composers, whether they are
writing vocal or instrumental music, are liable to have their
imagination prompted by some idea which to start with is only
incidental and may even appear irrelevant. The illustration of an
aria must also be governed by canons of taste: pictorial illustration is likely to sound naive, unless it is carefully integrated into
the whole, and any emphasis on individual words will seriously
disrupt the unity of the composition. The proper place for
detailed expression is not the aria but recitative, since here there
are no guiding lines, no formal structure, but only an imitation
of dramatic speech. Here Bach could be as definite and as
moving as any of his contemporaries, though in his harmony
he is generally less adventurous than composers like Handel and
Carl Heinrich Graun, whose Passion cantata *Der Tod Jesu* was
first performed in 1755.

The casual listener might think that the composition of recitative was an equally casual task for eighteenth-century composers, but this is a misunderstanding of their responsibility. It is true that they had ready to hand a whole collection of melodic formulas, and the sequence of diminished seventh chords in pathetic passages was so familiar that it did not need to be invented. But the application of the right phrase to the right words, and the proper accentuation of those words, was not a foregone conclusion. It is significant that Mattheson devotes a special section of his instruction to the composition of recitatives, taking a sample text, showing how each sentence should be set, and indicating where the rests should occur. Whatever criticisms can be brought against Bach's declamation in his arias there is no fault to be found with his recitatives. It is only when the text suggests a more ample mode of expression than mere recitation can offer that he allows himself the luxury of expanding the music, for instance in 'Ach wie flüchtig, ach wie nichtig' (BWV 26):

EX. 23

(Joy turns to sorrow)

where the contrast is expressed by a vivid *coloratura* on '*Freude*' and a diminished seventh chord on '*Traurigkeit*'.

Only two of Bach's cantatas appeared in print in his lifetime, and they were both youthful works (see p. 8). The first to be published after his death was 'Ein feste Burg' (BWV 80) in 1821, followed by a mere handful of others, including the *Coffee Cantata* and the *Peasant Cantata* in 1837. It was not until the foundation of the Bach-Gesellschaft in 1850 that the systematic publication of all Bach's works was undertaken. The very first volume, issued in 1851, was devoted to church cantatas – beginning, appropriately enough, with 'Wie schön leuchtet der Morgenstern' (BWV 1). By the time its labours came to an end in 1900 the society had published all the cantatas, both sacred and secular, that were then available, including some that were not by Bach at all. The publication of all these works was an invitation to performance; but nineteenth-century performance was often marred by errors of taste, including the addition of extra instruments, which we should find deplorable at the present day. We now know a good deal more about Bach's music; but there are still problems of interpretation, which are to be solved more by studying the music than by an industrious perusal of the theorists, and too often infelicities in performance which could be avoided by the exercise of intelligence. One of these is the habit of singing all recitatives very slowly, as though some ponderous message were being delivered. Except where there is a significant orchestral accompaniment, or where the melodic line calls for a spacious delivery, they should be sung at the speed at which they would be spoken by an experienced actor. There are even some which call for the utmost excitement, e.g. in 'Wachet auf' (BWV 140), where the tenor announces the arrival of the bridegroom:

> Er kommt, er kommt, der Bräut'gam kommt!
> Ihr Töchter Zions, kommt heraus,
> Sein Ausgang eilet aus der Höhe
>   In euer Mutter Haus.
> Der Braut'gam kommt, der einem Rehe
> Und jungen Hirsche gleich auf denen Hügeln springt,
> Und euch das Mahl der Hochzeit bringt.
> Wacht auf, ermuntert euch! den Bräut'gam zu empfangen.
>   Dort! sehet! kommt er hergegangen.

(He comes, he comes, the bridegroom comes! Daughters of Zion, come forth, he hastens from above to reach your mother's house. The bridegroom comes, leaping on the hills like a roe or a young stag, and brings you the wedding feast. Awake, rouse yourselves to greet the bridegroom. See, here he comes.)

Whatever the nature of the recitative, it is important that the organ accompaniment should not create a stodgy background through being obstinately sustained. Contemporary theorists agree that the chords in the right hand, at least, should be detached after being played, so that there is no interference with the singer's declamation.[1] Another matter which cannot be decided by any rule of thumb is the tempo of arias and choruses. Here the words must be studied as well as the music before any decision can be reached, and in making that decision it is

[1] The evidence is presented by Arthur Mendel, 'On the Keyboard Accompaniments to Bach's Leipzig Church Music', in *The Musical Quarterly*, xxxvi (1950), pp. 339–62.

important to consider not merely the voice parts but also what is happening in the orchestra.

In 1802 Johann Nicolaus Forkel, director of music at the University of Göttingen, published a biography of Bach – the first time that anyone had attempted a serious study of the composer's life and work. In his final chapter, devoted to a general appreciation, he wrote:

> His music is not merely agreeable, like other composers', but transports us to the regions of the ideal. It does not arrest our attention momentarily but grips us the stronger the oftener we listen to it, so that after a thousand hearings its treasures are still unexhausted and yield fresh beauties to excite our wonder. Even the beginner who knows but the A B C of his art warms with pleasure when he hears Bach's music and can open his ear and heart to it.[1]

This is still true today. It is a paradox of art that what was undertaken from necessity can stir our emotions as strongly as anything prompted merely by the artist's inclination to create. In fulfilling a routine which must often have been tedious, and sometimes intolerable, Bach not only satisfied the demands of his own age: he enriched our own.

---

[1] *Johann Sebastian Bach: his Life, Art and Work*, translated by C. S Terry (London, 1920), p. 151.